A New True Book

NORTH AMERICA

By D. V. Georges

CHILDRENS PRESS ®

CHICAGO

Northern fringe of the Great Salt Lake, Utah

PHOTO CREDITS

© Cameramann International, Ltd.—18 (center and right), 19, 21 (right), 27 (left), 35 (right), 40 (left), 44 (left)

Gartman Agency:
©Lee Balterman—18 (left)
©Frank Siteman—16 (top right)

© Virginia Grimes—37 (right)

Historical Pictures Service, Chicago—10 (3 photos)

Nawrocki Stock Photo: © Jeff Apoian—26, 38 (right)

Odyssey Productions, Chicago: © Bob Frerck—14 (right), 40 (right), 44 (right

Photri: © Gunvor Jorgsholm—30 (right)

R/C Photo Agency: © Richard L. Capps—23 (right)

© H. Armstrong Roberts—41 (left), Camerique—16 (top left)

Root Resources:
© James Blank—23 (left)
© Kitty Kohout—37 (left)
© Alan G. Nelson—31 (right)

© James P. Rowan—16 (bottom right)

© Bob & Ira Spring—Cover, 33 (left)

Tom Stack & Associates:
© W. Perry Conway—30 (left)
© John Gerlach—39 (left)
© Adrienne T. Gibson—42 (left)
© Dale Johnson—35 (left)
© Leonard Lee Rue III—32 (left)
© Sheryl S. McNee—21 (left)
© Brian Parker—25 (left)
© Tom Stack—31 (left)
© Gary K. Thompson—37 (center)

© Stock Imagery—25 (right)

Valan Photos:
© Kennon Cooke—39 (right)
© John Fowler—32 (right)
© Jean-Marie Jro—17 (left), 42 (right)
© M.G. Kingshott—2, 26 (right)
© Chris Malazdrewicz—15
© Denis Roy—33 (right)
© Wayne Shiels—27 (right)

Maps: Al Magnus—4, 7, 9, 13, 14, 17, 20, 24, 28, 34, 38, 41, 45

Cover: Gardens of Chateau Lake Louise, Banff National Park, Alberta, Canada

Library of Congress Cataloging-in-Publication Data

Georges, D.V.
  North America.

  (A New true book)
  Includes index.
  Summary: Identifies the continent of North America, divides it into six regions including the Eastern Seaboard, Great Lakes, Arctic Circle, and Central America, and discusses their countries, states, cities, and geographical features.
  1. North America—Description and travel—Juvenile literature. [1. North America—Description and travel] I. Title.
E41.G46 1986   970   86-9638
ISBN 0-516-01294-0

TABLE OF CONTENTS

Finding North America...5

Explorers of the New World...8

The Eastern Seaboard...14

Five Great Lakes...19

The Great Plains...24

Around the Arctic Circle...28

The North American Cordillera...34

Central America...40

Resources of a Continent...43

Words You Should Know...46

Index...47

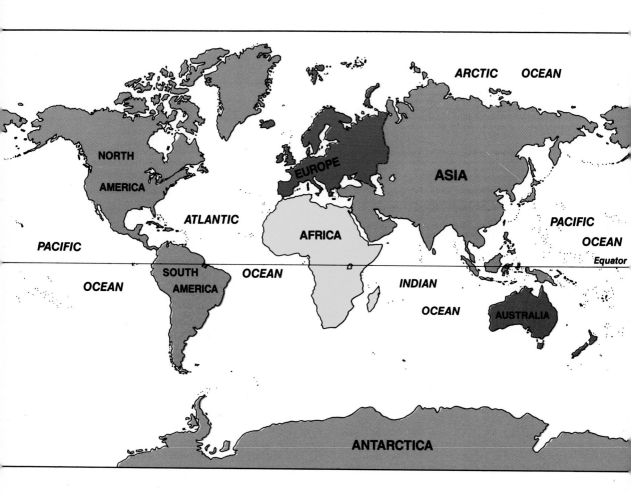

ARCTIC OCEAN

NORTH
AMERICA

ATLANTIC

PACIFIC

OCEAN

SOUTH
AMERICA

OCEAN

EUROPE

AFRICA

ASIA

PACIFIC

OCEAN

Equator

INDIAN

OCEAN

AUSTRALIA

ANTARCTICA

4

FINDING NORTH AMERICA

The seven continents are Asia, Africa, North America, South America, Antarctica, Europe, and Australia. They are the largest areas of land on earth.

North America and South America are in the Western Hemisphere—the western half of the earth.

Only a narrow strip of land connects North

America to South America.
It is called the Isthmus of
Panama.

Thousands of miles of
ocean border North
America. The Pacific
Ocean lies to the west, the
Atlantic Ocean to the east.
And far to the north is the
icy Arctic Ocean.

North America is the
third-largest continent.
Greenland, Canada, the
United States, Mexico,

Central America, and the
West Indies are part of
North America.

EXPLORERS OF THE NEW WORLD

The Vikings were the first explorers to reach North America. From Europe they sailed the waters of the North Atlantic. In A.D. 982, Eric the Red discovered Greenland. He and his followers settled there.

Much later, Christopher Columbus set sail from Spain. He believed the

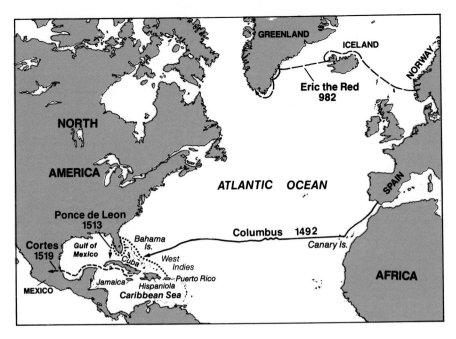

earth was round. By sailing
west, he hoped to find
Asia. He was looking for a
shorter route to the wealth
of India and the Far East.

Columbus never reached
Asia. But his voyages
across the Atlantic began
a new period of history.

Columbus (left), Juan Ponce de Leon (middle), and Hernando Cortes (right), were among the first Europeans to explore North America.

Explorers from many countries followed.

Columbus first sailed in 1492. His ships landed in the West Indies, a chain of islands between Florida and Venezuela. They separate the Atlantic Ocean from the Caribbean Sea.

Soon after Columbus, people from Spain settled on the largest West Indies islands—Cuba, Hispaniola, and Jamaica. From there they set out to conquer other parts of the "New World" of North and South America.

In 1508, Juan Ponce de Leon conquered Puerto Rico. Five years later, he discovered Florida.

Hernando Cortes conquered Mexico. He

fought two long battles with the Aztec Indians there. In 1520, Cortes defeated the Aztec emperor Montezuma.

The English and French explored much farther north. Only a few years after Columbus sailed, John Cabot discovered Newfoundland. In 1524, the French explorer Jacques Cartier discovered the Saint Lawrence River.

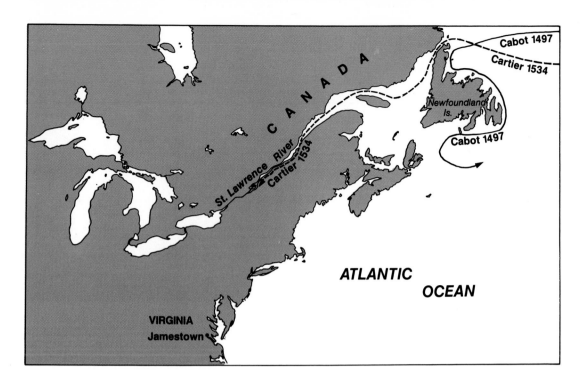

Almost one hundred
years passed before
settlers came. In the early
1600s, English settlers
founded Jamestown,
Virginia. French fur traders
and missionaries settled in
Canada.

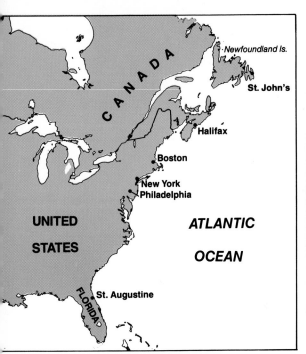

Harbor at Halifax, Canada

THE EASTERN SEABOARD

A seaboard is land that borders a coast. In North America, the eastern seaboard borders the Atlantic Ocean. It stretches from Florida to the island

Saint John's in Newfoundland, Canada

of Newfoundland in
Canada.

Many cities are along
the eastern seaboard. In
Canada, Halifax and Saint
John's have beautiful
natural harbors. Cod fishing
is one of the main
industries of these cities.

Left: Downtown Philadelphia, Pennsylvania. Top right: Aerial view of Boston, Massachusett. Bottom right: The oldest house in St. Augustine, Florida

In the United States, Philadelphia, New York City, and Boston are centers for culture and industry. They are also busy ports.

Saint Augustine, Florida, is the oldest city in the

New York, New York

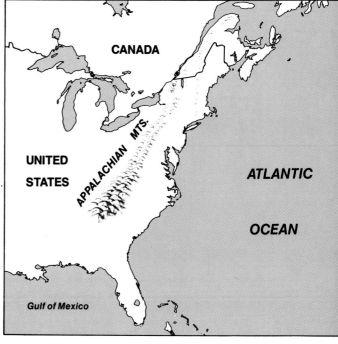

CANADA

UNITED STATES

APPALACHIAN MTS.

ATLANTIC

OCEAN

Gulf of Mexico

United States. There are several historic Spanish-style buildings in Saint Augustine.

The Appalachian Mountains are inland from the eastern seaboard. They extend from Canada to

Left: Coal miners in West Virginia. Center: Harvesting cotton in Georgia. Right: Picking grapefruit in Florida

Alabama. The Appalachian Mountains are rich in coal.

Near the mountains there is good farmland. In the southeast United States, farmers grow peanuts and cotton. Citrus fruit grows in Florida.

Skyline view of Chicago, Illinois near Lake Michigan.

FIVE GREAT LAKES

West of the Atlantic seaboard lie the five Great Lakes.

Four of the Great Lakes form a border between Canada and the United States.

Many important cities have been founded on the shores of the lakes. Milwaukee and Chicago

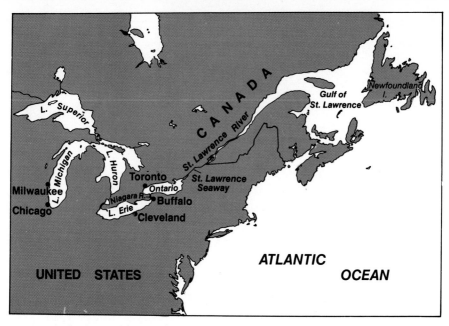

Of the Great Lakes, only Lake Michigan
lies completely within the United States.

are on Lake Michigan.
Cleveland and Buffalo are
on Lake Erie.

One of the largest cities
in Canada—Toronto—is on
the north shore of Lake
Ontario.

The Saint Lawrence is

Left: Lake Ontario in Toronto, Canada. Right: Saint
Lambert Lock on the Saint Lawrence River in Montreal, Canada

an important river of the
Great Lakes region. It
flows from Lake Ontario to
the Gulf of Saint Lawrence,
which opens to the Atlantic
Ocean.

Rivers join some of the
Great Lakes. Where there

21

are no rivers, canals have been built to connect the lakes. Because of the rivers and canals, ships from all of the Great Lakes can reach the Atlantic.

The Niagara River joins Lake Erie with Lake Ontario. It forms part of the United States-Canada border.

The Niagara River is only thirty-five miles long!

The magnificent Niagara Falls are on the Niagara

The Horseshoe Falls (left) are on the Canadian side of the Niagara River.
The Niagara Falls (right) are on the American side.

River where the river drops 160 feet.

Goat Island is a small island that divides the falls in two. The Horseshoe Falls are in Canada. The American Falls are in the United States.

THE GREAT PLAINS

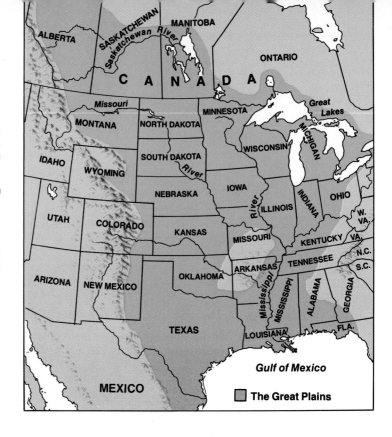

The Great Plains are in the central part of North America. They stretch from north Canada to Texas. East to west, the Great Plains are several hundred miles wide.

Fields of wheat and corn are
harvested each year.

Fields of corn and wheat
cover the plains. Because
so much wheat grows, the
Great Plains are sometimes
called "the breadbasket of
North America."

There are many cattle
ranches in the Great Plains.

Left: Montana sheep farm. Right: The Missouri River
winding through mountains in Montana

Sheep are also raised.

In a few areas, the land
is hilly. Low mountains rise
out of the plains in North
Dakota and Montana.

The Missouri River flows
through the Great Plains
from Montana to Missouri.
It joins the Mississippi River
in eastern Missouri. The

Left: Mississippi River Delta, south of
New Orleans. Above: South
Saskatchewan River at Saskatoon,
Saskatchewan

Missouri is the longest
branch of the Mississippi River.
In Canada, the
Saskatchewan River flows
through the Great Plains.
The North and South
Saskatchewan rivers meet in
the Province of Saskatchewan.

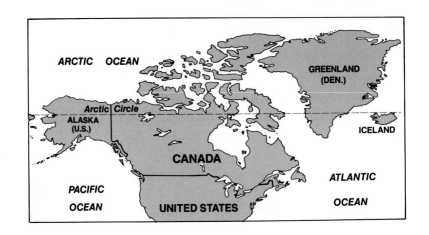

AROUND THE ARCTIC CIRCLE

Greenland is the largest island in the world. It is an overseas state of Denmark, in Europe. Hundreds of smaller islands called the Arctic Islands are west of Greenland. They are part of Canada.

The Arctic Circle passes

through Greenland, Canada, and Alaska. The Arctic Circle is an imaginary circle. Every point on it is 1,500 miles from the North Pole.

Winter temperatures near the Arctic Circle are below freezing, but summer temperatures are much warmer.

In the Greenland interior, summer temperatures remain below freezing. A huge ice sheet that covers

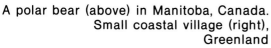
A polar bear (above) in Manitoba, Canada.
Small coastal village (right),
Greenland

most of Greenland keeps
temperatures cold.

Polar bears and Arctic
foxes live near the Arctic
Circle. Polar bears have
white fur that helps them
blend in with the snow. For
the same reason—
protection—the Arctic fox

Artic fox (left)
Alaskan fur seal (above)

has fur that changes color with the seasons. In summer, the fur is gray; in winter, it is white or blue-gray.

Thousand of seals and walruses live on Arctic shores. The walrus is a relative of the seal.

Walrus bull (above) sunning itself.
Eskimo fisherman (right) on Baffin Island

Walruses can weigh up to
3,000 pounds! They use
their long ivory tusks to
dig up clams from the sea
bottom.

Most of the people of
the Arctic are Eskimo.
They hunt seals, whales,
and walrus. They also fish.

32

King Island Eskimo girl and brother (left)
Airplanes and snowmobiles have replaced
dog sleds.

In the past, the Eskimo
were known for their igloos
made of snow blocks. But
they made only a few
igloos of snow. Many more
igloos were of clay and
wood. Most Eskimo today
live in modern houses.

THE NORTH AMERICAN CORDILLERA

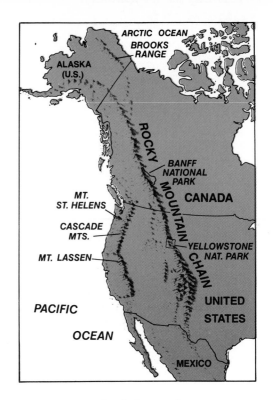

The west part of North America is mountainous. Several mountain chains lie between the Pacific coast and the Great Plains. To the south, mountains cover much of Mexico and Central America. The

Left: Brooks Range, Alaska
Above: Pikes Peak, Colorado

mountain chains are called
the North American
Cordillera.

The Rockies are the
longest mountain chain in
the cordillera. They begin
in northern Alaska, where
they are called the Brooks
Range.

There are many national parks in the rugged and scenic Rockies. In Canada, Banff National Park is full of ice fields and mountain lakes. In the United States, Yellowstone is the oldest and best known of the national parks.

Yellowstone has thousands of geysers, hot springs, and waterfalls. Hot underground water flows to the earth's surface in hot springs. Geysers erupt when the hot underground

Left: Banff National Park, Canada. Center: "Old Faithful Geyser,"
Yellowstone National Park, Wyoming. Right: Mount Lassen Peak, California

water has turned to steam.
West of the Rockies, the
Cascade Mountains cross
Washington and Oregon.
Mount Saint Helens and
Mount Lassen are
volcanoes of the Cascades.

Death Valley in California

Between the Rockies
and the California part of
the cordillera is the Great
Basin region.

Death Valley, the Great
Salt Lake, and the Grand
Canyon are in the Great
Basin. Mountains to the
east and west keep rain

Left: The Grand Canyon, Arizona.
Right: Sierra Madre in Mexico

out of the Great Basin.
Much of it is dry and hot.
The Mohave Desert lies to
the south.

In Mexico, the mountain
chains are called the Sierra
Madre. As in the Great Basin,
land between the mountains
is dry and hot.

CENTRAL AMERICA

Ship awaiting passage through the Panama Canal
Far right: A farmer harvests cocoa.

Central America is south of Mexico. The countries of Central America are Belize, Guatemala, El Salvador, Honduras, Nicaragua, Costa Rica, and Panama.

The Isthmus of Panama covers all of Panama. The

Izalco Volcano, El Salvador

Panama Canal connects the Pacific Ocean with the Caribbean Sea.

There are many volcanoes in the mountains of Central America. Land near the mountains is fertile. Farmers grow and export coffee, cocoa, and bananas.

Above: Maya ruins at Campeche, Mexico.
Right: Women of Atitlán Lake, Guatemala

Maya Indians live in
southern Mexico,
Guatemala, and Honduras.
The ancient Maya were
astronomers and sculptors.
Ruins of their beautiful
temples still stand.

RESOURCES OF A CONTINENT

North America has made much progress since the first settlers came to the New World. The many resources of the continent helped make such progress possible.

Large areas of land in North America are good for farming. In many other areas, cattle and sheep are raised. The mountains are rich in important minerals.

North America has a rich but limited supply of natural resources.

Most countries of North America are oil producers. Oil has been found as far north as the Arctic Circle and as far south as Mexico and Central America.

Settlers—past and present— of North America have found opportunity in this land of many resources.

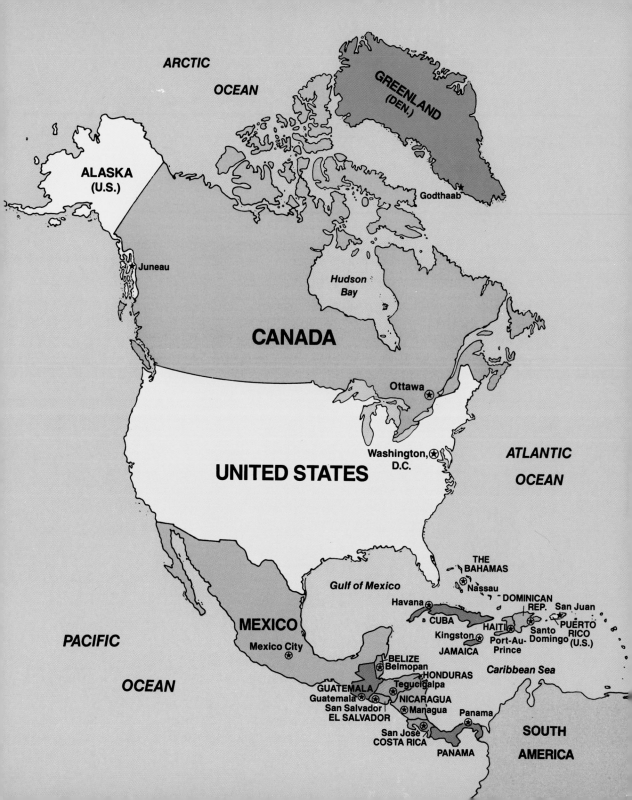

WORDS YOU SHOULD KNOW

canal(kuh • NAL) — a channel built on land to connect two bodies of water

citrus fruit(SIT • iss FROOT) — the family of fruit that includes lemons, limes, oranges, and grapefruit

fertile(FUR • til) — capable of growing plants

geyser(GYE • zer) — a fountain of steam from underground that erupts on the earth's surface

igloo(IHG • loo) — an Eskimo house, originally built from blocks of snow

inland(IN • land) — away from the coast or border of a place

interior(in • TEER • ree • yer) — land that is inside a country's coasts or borders

isthmus(ISS • miss) — a narrow strip of land that connects two larger bodies of land

missionaries(MISH • un • air • eez) — people who travel to distant lands to teach the Christian religion

mountainous(MOUN • tin • uss) — having many mountains

North Pole(NORTH POAL) — an imaginary geographical point at the top of the earth

plateau(plat • OH) — a broad flatland that can have a high elevation

port(PORT) — a city on a sea or river where ships dock

province(PRAH • vince) — a division of a country that is similar to a state

seaboard(SEE • bord) — a region that borders the sea or ocean

Vikings(VYE • kings) — people of Scandinavia, in northern Europe, who sailed the oceans and conquered new lands

volcano(vawl • KANE • oh) — a mountain that sometimes erupts with melted rock and steam

MAJOR COUNTRIES IN NORTH AMERICA

Name	Date of Independence	Capital	Name	Date of Independence	Capital
Anguilia (British dependency)			Jamaica	1962	Kingston
Antigua and Barbuda	1981	St. John's	Martinique (France)		Fort-de-France
Bahamas	1973	Nassau	Montserrat (British)		Plymouth
Barbados	1966	Bridgetown	Mexico	1821	Mexico City
Belize	1981	Belmopan	Netherlands Antilles		Willemstad
Bermuda (British dependency)		Hamilton	Nicaragua	1821	Managua
Canada	1931	Ottawa	Panama	1903	Panama City
Cayman Islands (British dependency)		Georgetown	Puerto Rico (United States commonwealth)		San Juan
Costa Rica	1821	San Jose	St. Christopher and Nevis	1983	Basseterre
Cuba	1898	Havana	St. Lucia	1979	Castries
Dominica	1978	Roseau	St. Pierre and Miquelon (France)		St. Pierre
Dominican Republic	1844	Santo Domingo	St. Vincent and the		
El Salvador	1821	San Salvador	Grenadines	1979	Kingstown
Greenland (Province of Denmark)		Godthaab	Trinidad and Tobago	1962	Port-of-Spain
Grenada	1974	Saint George's	Turks and Caicos Islands (British dependency)		Grand Turk
Guadeloupe (France)		Basse-Terre	United States of America	1776	Washington, D.C.
Guatemala	1821	Guatemala City	Virgin Islands (U.S.)		Charlotte Amalie/ St. Thomas
Haiti	1804	Port-au-Prince			
Honduras	1821	Tegucigalpa	Virgin Islands (British)		Road Town

INDEX

Africa, 5

Alabama, 18

Alaska, 29, 35

American Falls, 23

Antarctica, 5

Appalachian Mountains, 17, 18

Arctic Circle, 28-30, 45

Arctic foxes, 30, 31

Arctic Ocean, 6

Asia, 5, 9

Atlantic Ocean, 6, 8-10, 14, 21, 22

Australia, 5

Aztec Indians, 12

Banff National Park, 36

Belize, 40

Brooks Range, 35

Cabot, John, 12

California, 38

Canada, 6, 13, 15, 17, 19, 20, 22, 23, 24, 27, 28, 36

Caribbean Sea, 10, 41

Cartier, Jacques, 12

Cascade Mountains, 37

Central America, 7, 34, 40-42, 44

Columbus, Christopher, 8-11

Cortes, Hernando, 11, 12

Costa Rica, 40

Cuba, 11

Death Valley, 38

Denmark, 28

eastern seaboard, 14-18

El Salvador, 40

Eric the Red, 8

Eskimo people, 32, 33

Europe, 5, 8, 28

Far East, 9

Florida, 10, 11, 14, 16, 18

Goat Island, 23

Grand Canyon, 38

Great Basin, 38, 39

Great Lakes, 19-22
Great Plains, 24-27, 34
Great Salt Lake, 38
Greenland, 6, 8, 28-30
Guatemala, 40, 42
Gulf of Saint Lawrence, 21
Honduras, 40, 42
igloos, 33
India, 9
Isthmus of Panama, 6, 40
Jamaica, 11
Lake Erie, 20, 22
Lake Michigan, 20
Lake Ontario, 20, 21, 22
Maya Indians, 42
Mexico, 6, 11, 34, 39, 40, 42, 44
Mississippi River, 26, 27
Missouri River, 26, 27
Mohave Desert, 39
Montana, 26
Montezuma, 12
Mount Lassen, 37
Mount Saint Helens, 37
Newfoundland, 12, 15
"New World," 11, 43
Niagara Falls, 22, 23
Niagara River, 22, 23
Nicaragua, 40
North American Cordillera, 34-39
North Atlantic Ocean, 8
North Dakota, 26

North Pole, 29
North Saskatchewan River, 27
oil, 44
Oregon, 37
Pacific Ocean, 6, 41
Panama, 40
Panama, Isthmus of, 6, 40
Panama Canal, 41
polar bears, 30
Ponce de Leon, Juan, 11
Puerto Rico, 11
Rocky Mountains, 35-38
Saint Augustine, Florida, 16, 17
Saint Lawrence River, 12, 20
Saskatchewan (province), 27
Saskatchewan River, 27
seals, 31, 32
Sierra Madre, 39
South America, 5, 6, 11
Spain, 8, 11
Texas, 24
United States, 6, 16-19, 22, 23, 36
Venezuela, 10
Vikings, 8
Virginia, 13
walruses, 31, 32
Washington, 37
Western Hemisphere, 5
West Indies, 7, 10, 11
Yellowstone National Park, 36

About the author

D.V. Georges is a geophysicist in Houston, Texas. Dr. Georges attended Rice University, earning a masters degree in chemistry in 1975 and a doctorate in geophysics in 1978.

970
G

Georges, D. V.

North America

$19.00

DATE			